HOW TO USE THIS BOOK

You might be thinking, **"Seriously? It's a coloring book! Why would I need instructions?"**

And you would be right...**IF** this were just a coloring book.

However, what you now hold in your hands is far more powerful than a child's creative distraction or a relaxation tool for overstressed adults.

This book (cleverly disguised as a coloring book) is a highly effective tool designed to make your life better by making **you** better. (After all, you are the one constant in your life. Everywhere you go, there YOU are.)

As you flip through these pages to choose your next pattern to color, consider which attribute you'd like to have more of right now. Would you like to be more confident? More caring? More abundant?

By relaxing and coloring each page any way you choose, your subconscious mind can't help but absorb the "I can be" statement on that page. You couldn't stop it if you tried – your mind is **that** powerful.

What you think about, you bring about. **Patterns of Purpose** incorporates the relaxing repetition of pattern coloring to help you focus your mind on more of what and who YOU want to be.

So pick a page and dive right in to a better you.

ABOUT THE CREATOR OF THIS BOOK

AMY SCOTT GRANT, otherwise known as the Spiritual Ass Kicker, is a bestselling author, speaker, and human potential expert. She is a master intuitive healer who lives in Colorado with her husband and three children. If you like this book, be sure to visit Amy's website to collect your free healing gifts: **AskAmyAnything.com**

OTHER BOOKS BY AMY SCOTT GRANT

1-2-3 Clarity! Banish Your Blocks, Doubts, Fears, and Limiting Beliefs Like a Spiritual Badass
Pendulum Mojo: How to Use Truth Testing for Clarity, Confidence, and Peace of Mind
2016 Boom: The Personal Almanac System That Will Change Your Year

Published by Liberto Press
Castle Rock, Colorado, USA
© 2015 Amy Scott Grant
Book design, cover, and production by LibertoPress.com

All Rights Reserved. No part of this publication may be used reproduced or transmitted in any form or by any means, including informational storage and retrieval systems, without express written permission of the copyright holder.

ISBN: 978-0-9862269-7-7
First Liberto Press printing, October 2015

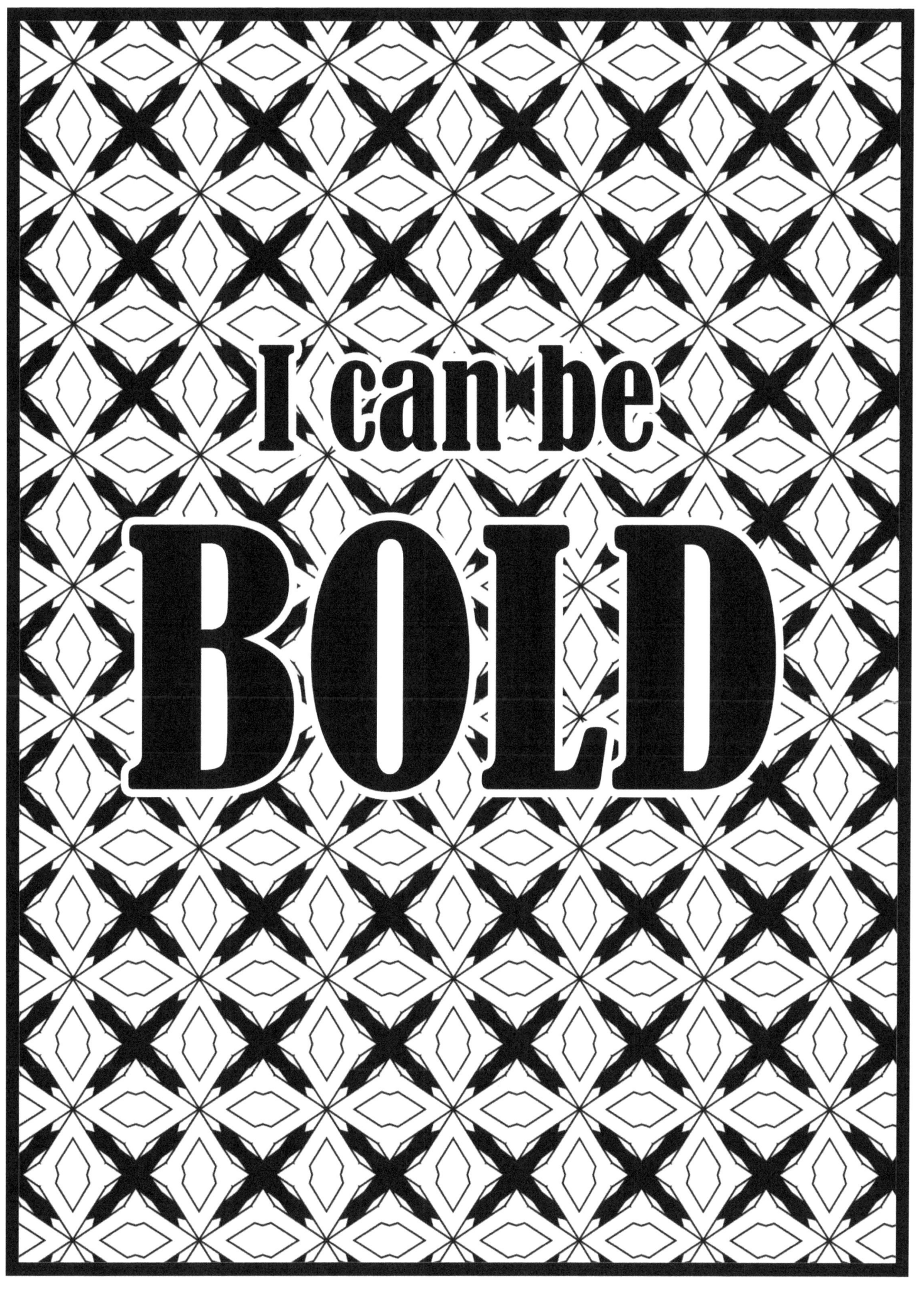

I can be... COURAGEOUS

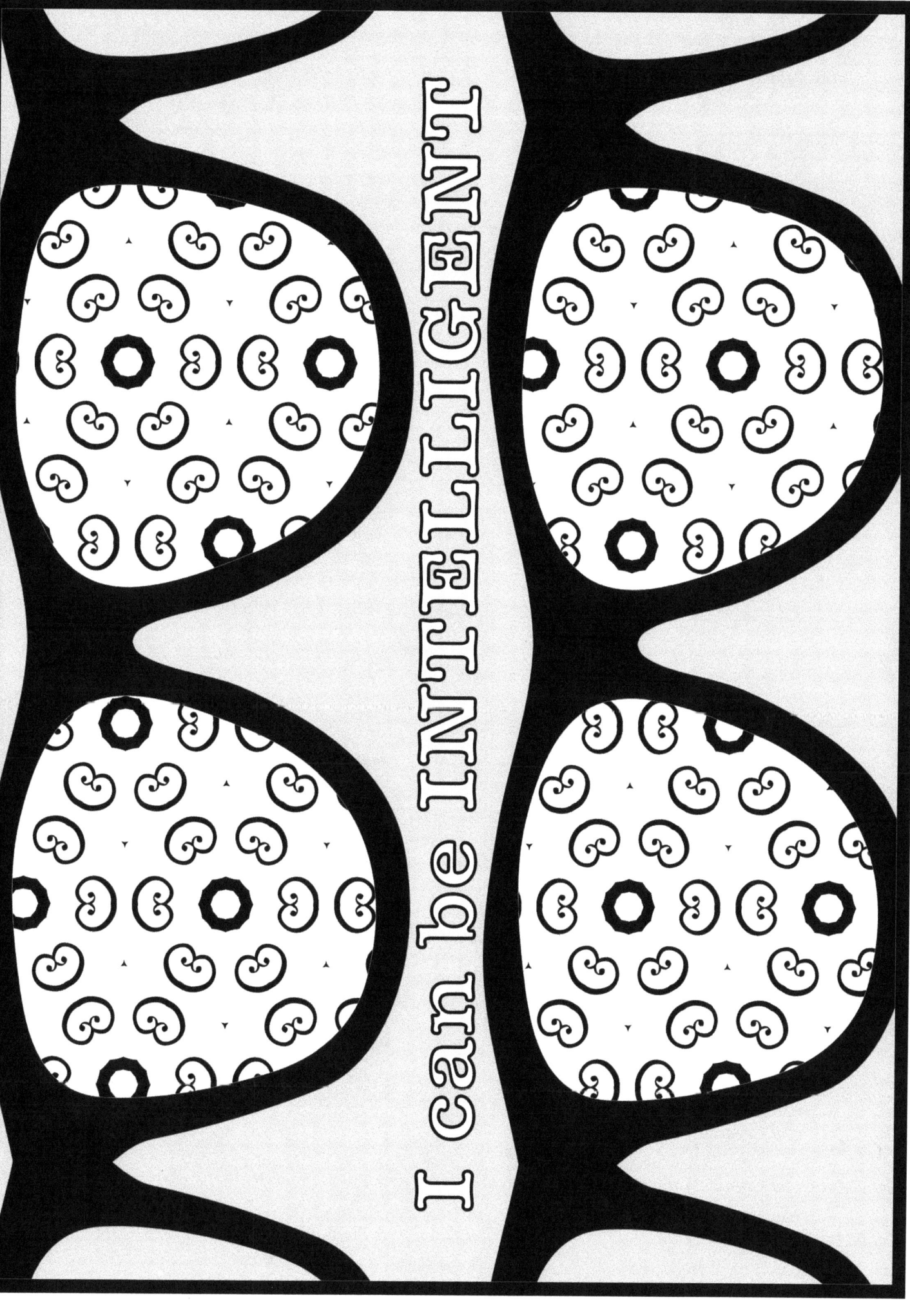

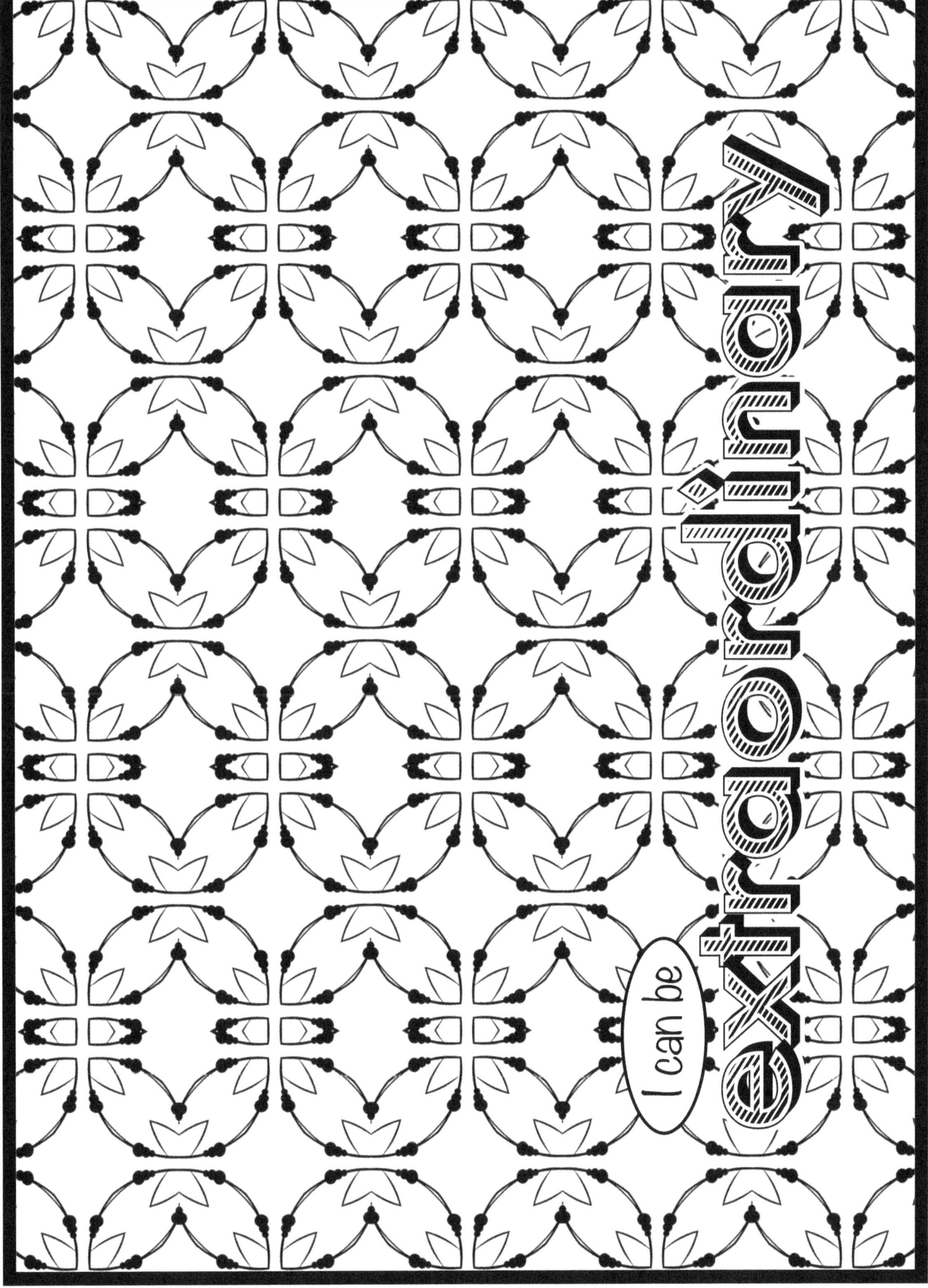

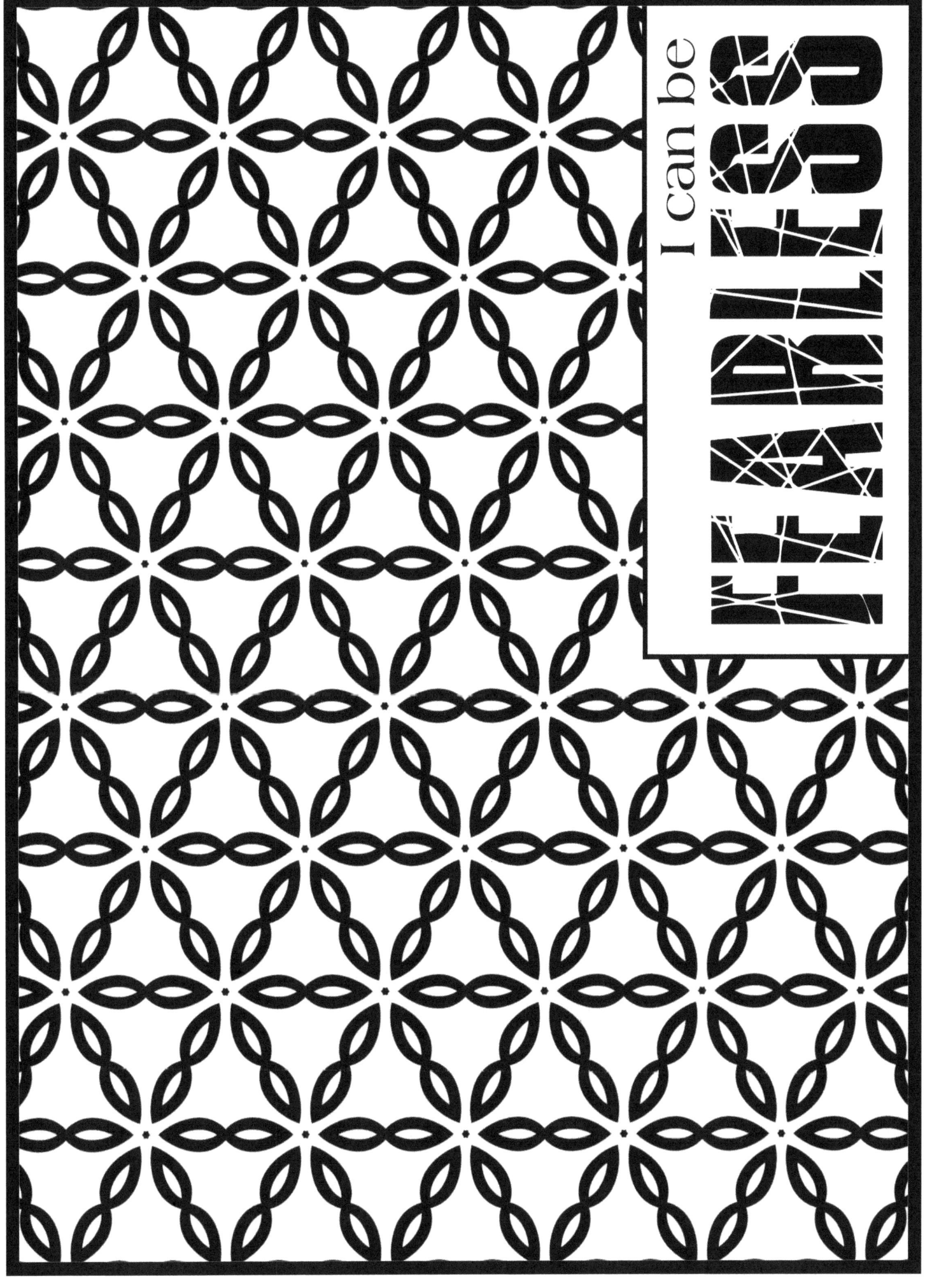

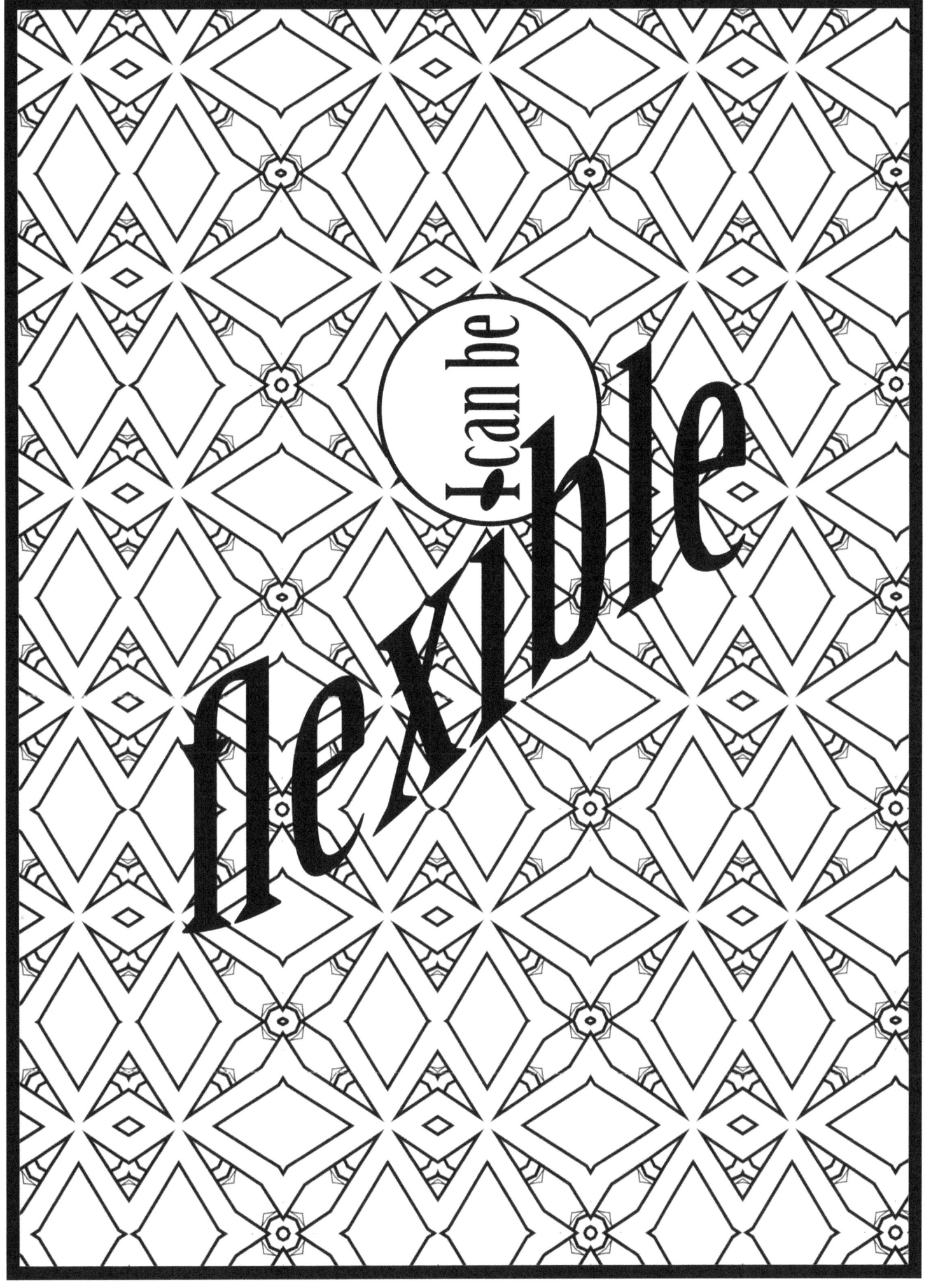

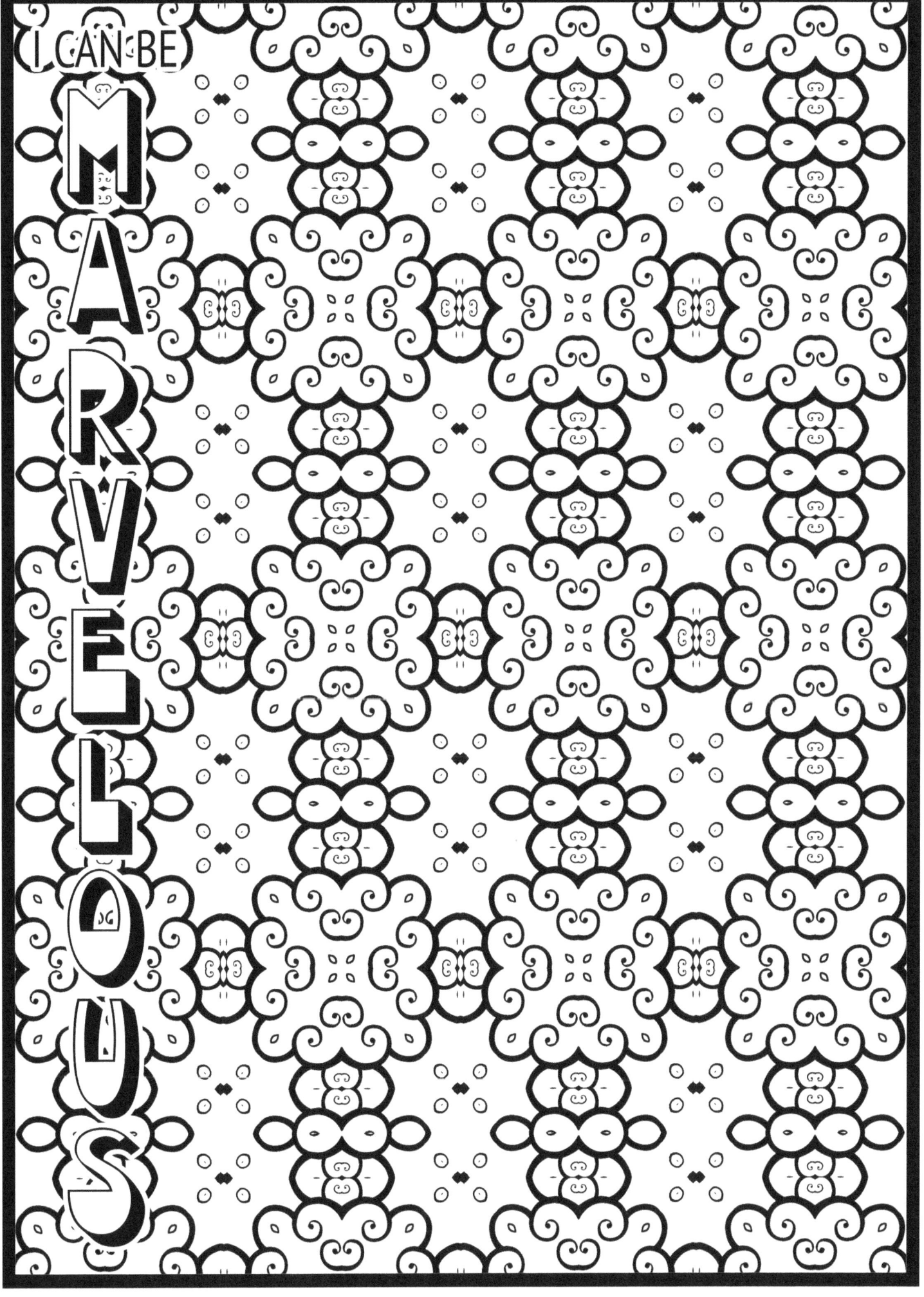

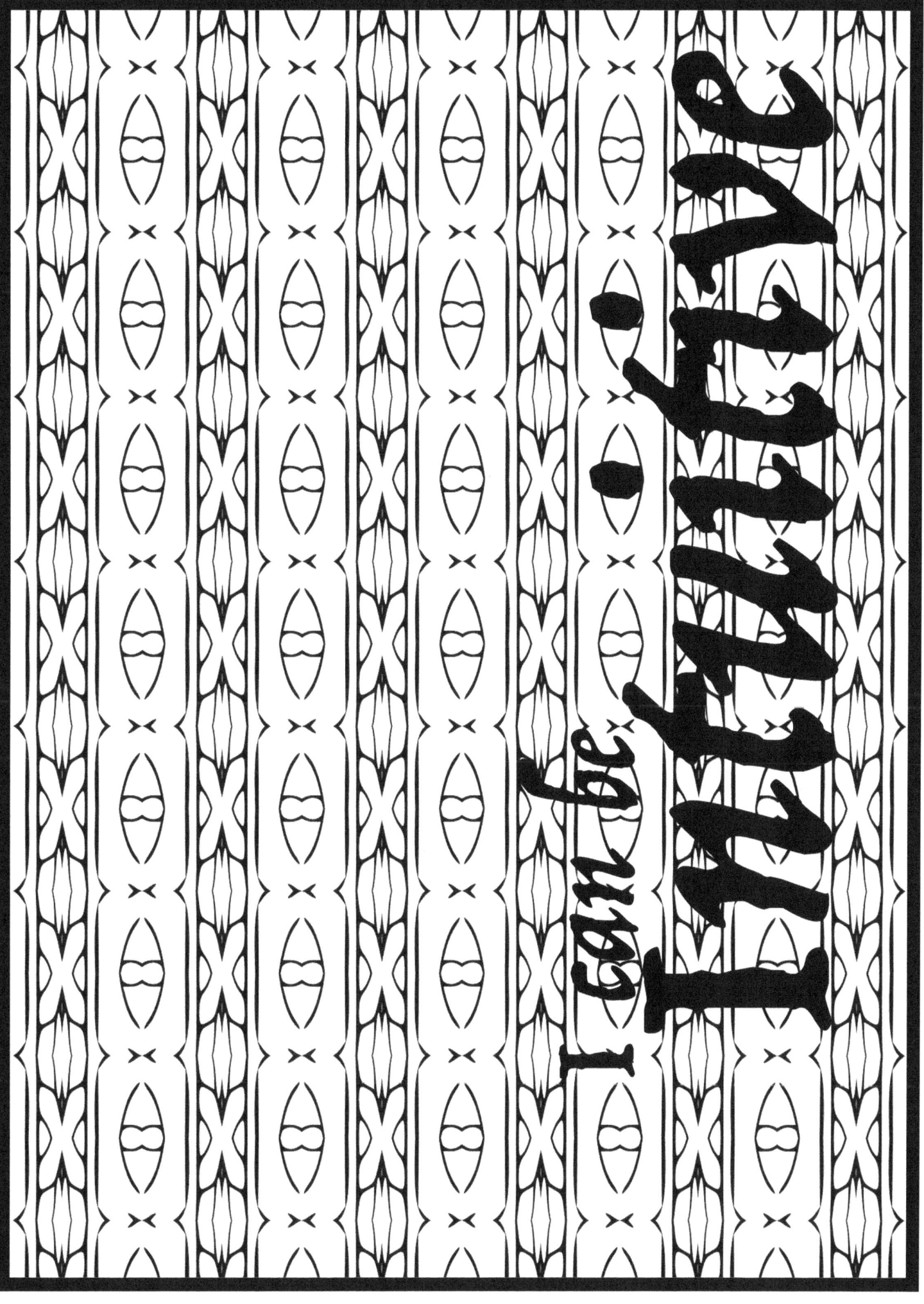

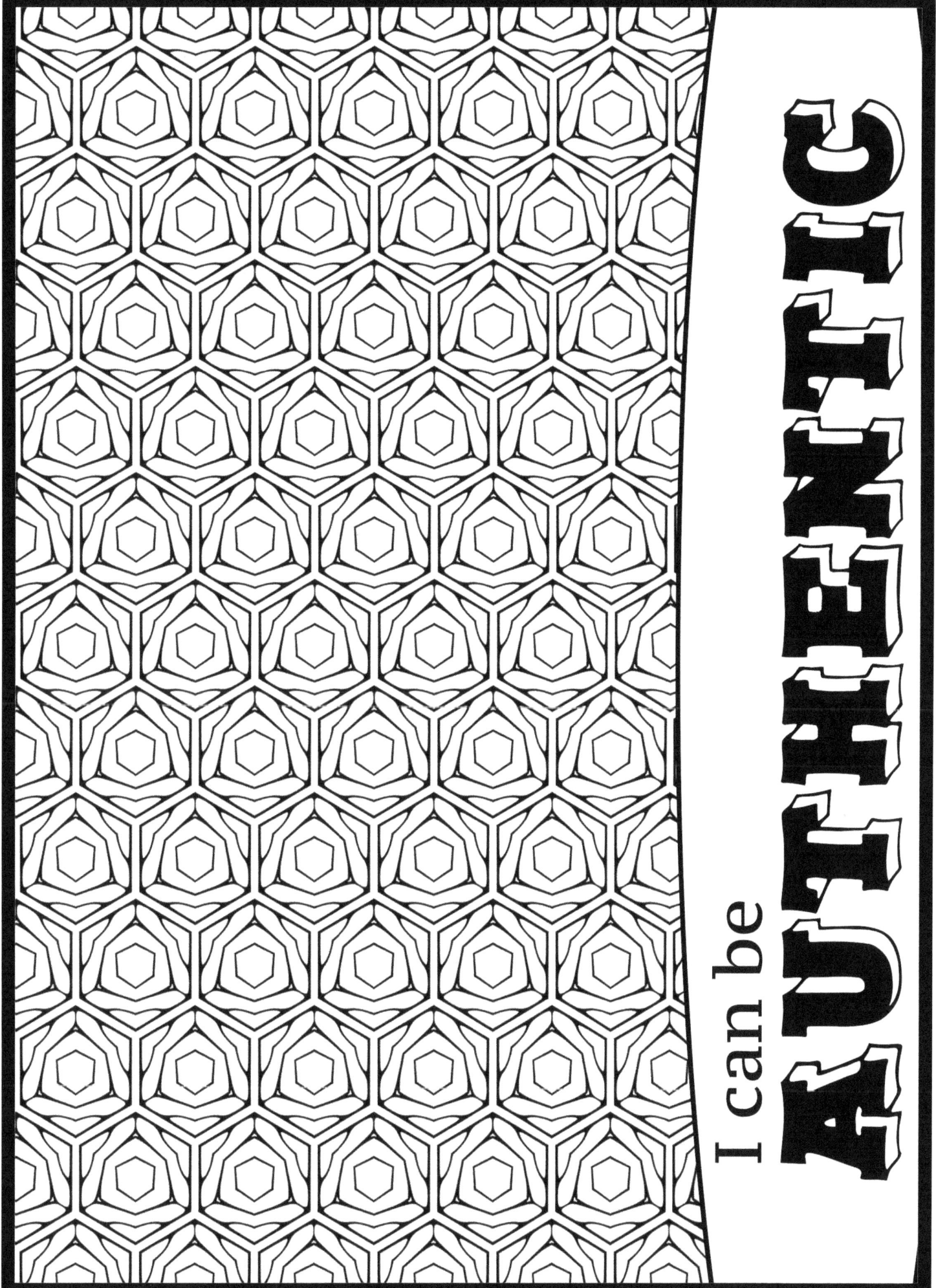

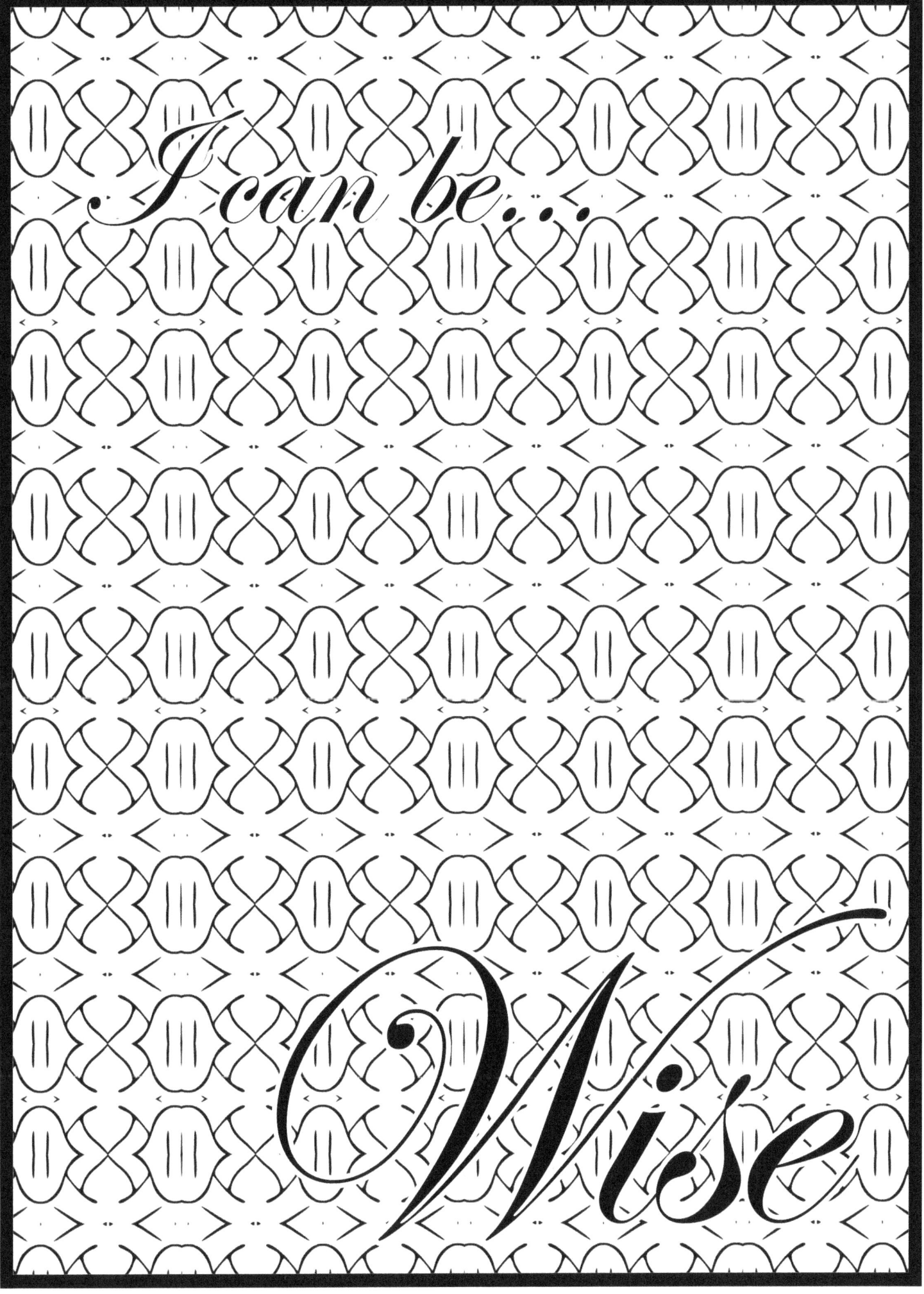

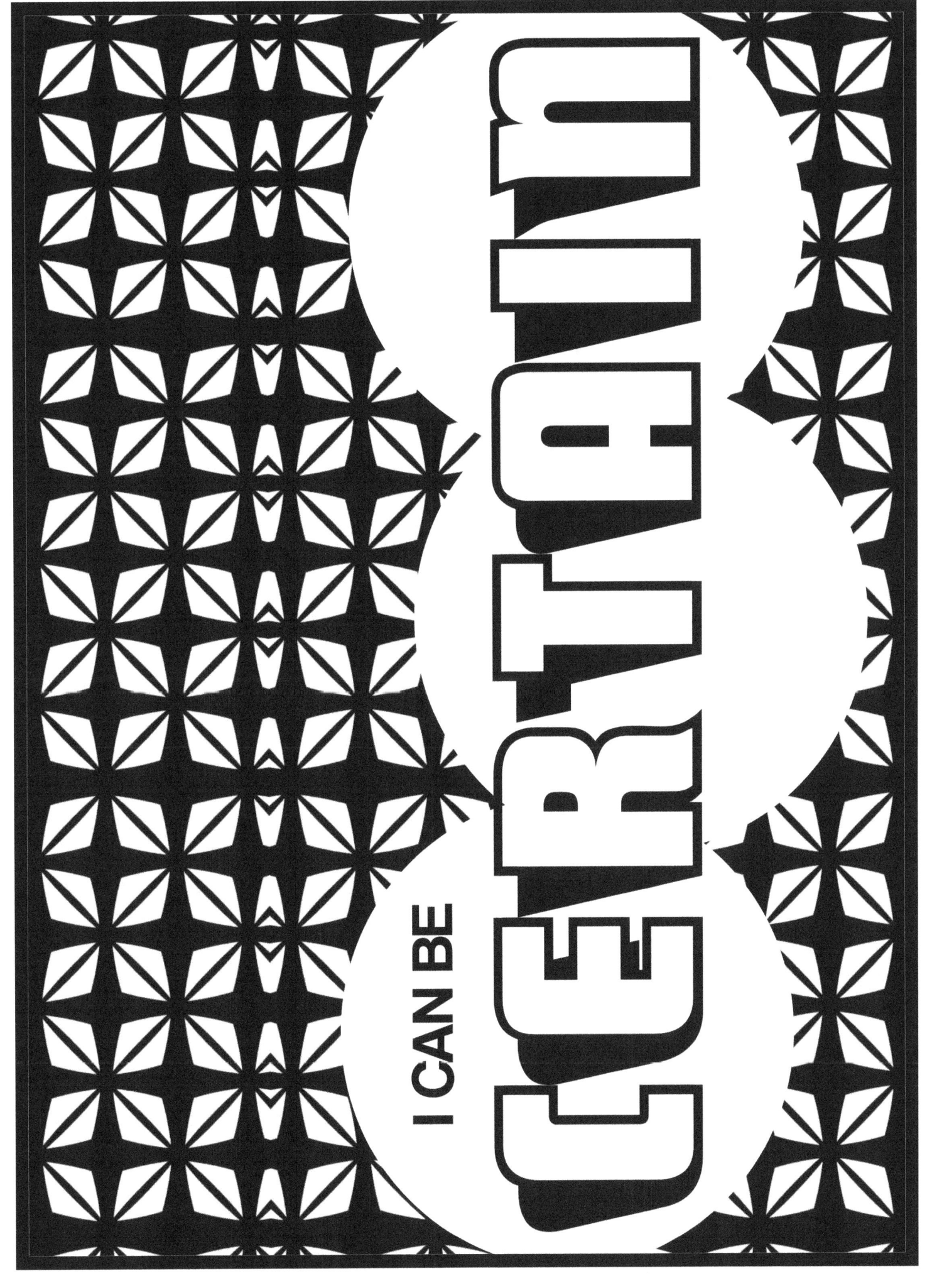

www.ingramcontent.com/pod-product-compliance
Lightning Source LLC
Chambersburg PA
CBHW081348040426
42450CB00015B/3346